# SINBAD

A Real-Life Reader Biography

Melanie Cole

**Mitchell Lane Publishers, Inc.**
P.O. Box 200 • Childs, Maryland 21916

First Printing

**Real-Life Reader Biographies**

| | | | |
|---|---|---|---|
| Selena | Robert Rodriguez | Mariah Carey | Rafael Palmeiro |
| Tommy Nuñez | Trent Dimas | Cristina Saralegui | Andres Galarraga |
| Oscar De La Hoya | Gloria Estefan | Jimmy Smits | Mary Joe Fernandez |
| Cesar Chavez | Chuck Norris | Sinbad | Paula Abdul |
| Vanessa Williams | Celine Dion | Mia Hamm | LeAnn Rimes |

Library of Congress Cataloging-in-Publication Data
Cole, Melanie, 1957–
    Sinbad / Melanie Cole.
       p. cm. — (A real-life reader biography)
    Includes index.
    Summary: A biography of the comedian Sinbad, who has starred in television shows and movies, written his autobiography, and performed benefits for Morehouse College, Bosnia, and AIDS awareness.
    ISBN 1-883845-73-4
    1. Sinbad, 1956– —Juvenile literature. 2. Comedians—United States—Biography—Juvenile literature. [1. Sinbad, 1956– . 2. Comedians. 3. Afro-Americans—Biography.] I. Title. II. Series.
PN2287.S392C66   1998
792.7'028'092—dc21
[B]
                                                                                98-38128
                                                                                      CIP
                                                                                       AC

**ABOUT THE AUTHOR: Melanie Cole** has been a writer and editor for eighteen years. She was previously an associate editor of *Texas Monthly* and then an editor of *Hispanic* magazine. She has published numerous poems, articles, and reviews. She is a contributing writer to the Mitchell Lane series **Famous People of Hispanic Heritage** and has authored several books for children, including **Mary Joe Fernandez** (Mitchell Lane) and **Jimmy Smits** (Mitchell Lane). Originally from Kansas, Ms. Cole now resides in Austin, Texas.
**PHOTO CREDITS:** cover: Globe Photos; p. 4 Diana Lyn/Shooting Star; p. 9 Harry Langdon/Shooting Star; p. 15 Diana Lyn/Shooting Star; p. 22 AP Photo; p. 25 Barry King/Shooting Star; p. 26 Terry Lilly/Shooting Star.
**ACKNOWLEDGMENTS:** The following story has been thoroughly researched, and to the best of our knowledge, represents a true story. Though we try to authorize every biography that we publish, for various reasons, this is not always possible.

# Table of Contents

## Chapter 1
# Wild Child

"People are always coming up to me and saying, 'Sinbad, you're so crazy, man. How do you do it?'

"I don't know how. There's a crazy gene that runs through my family that I must have been blessed with—mine is just more active than most. So whatever you do, don't try to be me. I am a *professional* crazy person," Sinbad tells his audience.

The comedian and actor known as Sinbad was born on

**"I am a profes-sional crazy person," Sinbad tells his audience.**

November 10, 1956, in Benton Harbor, Michigan. Benton Harbor is a medium-sized city on the coast of Lake Michigan, in the far southwest corner of the state. There Sinbad grew up, played basketball in the park, and attended Benton Harbor public schools. He was known as a prankster and entertainer from the moment he could stand up and talk.

His name is not really Sinbad. Sinbad is a name that he chose for himself when he was a teenager. His given name is David Adkins. He is the son of the Reverend Donald Adkins and Louise Adkins, who had a family of six children. His brother Donald Jr. is oldest, then David (Sinbad), sisters Dorothea and Donna, then brothers Michael and Mark. Sinbad grew up playing tricks on his brothers and sisters and telling them stories.

Young David Adkins liked the name Sinbad because he liked to think of himself as a hero who was also a trickster. When he was feeling bad about things that had happened or when times were hard, he would make himself feel better by thinking, "I'm Sinbad. . . . Sinbad doesn't give up. Sinbad goes the distance." Another thing that made the mythic character Sinbad attractive to him, he says, is that "he didn't have the strength of Hercules, but he could outwit anyone."

In Sinbad's book, *Sinbad's Guide to Life: Because I Know Everything,* published in 1997, he offered this explanation for why he chose the hero from the *Arabian Nights*:

**Young David Adkins liked the name Sinbad because he liked to think of himself as a hero who was also a trickster.**

> **Sometimes, Sinbad makes himself sound worse than he really was. He was also an A student.**

"You see, I always loved the character Sinbad, from the first time I saw him as a small kid back in Michigan on our old black-and-white television when they would run the old Douglas Fairbanks, Jr., movies after school. . . . I was so fascinated by Sinbad the Sailor that I scoured the library looking for any information I could find about him. . . . I sat in that library hour after hour, all by my goofy, gawky self trying to break down his adventures into words that I could understand."

Audiences can tell from the way Sinbad performs that he was fairly naughty as a child. The way he tells it in his comedy routines, he lied all the time to his parents, was sneaky, got his brothers and sisters in trouble, and was always getting "whuppings" from his parents. But no doubt Sinbad makes himself sound worse than he really was. He was also an A student who was labeled a nerd.

Actually, Sinbad was a mixture—part loyal, studious son and part crazy show-off. When he performs his comedy routines, you

*When Sinbad performs you can still see the wild child inside.*

can still see in him the wild kid, doing anything to get attention, acting silly, flying around in the Adkins household. Sinbad was the kind of kid who would act silly and basically do anything to get a laugh.

Sinbad's first love was basketball. He dreamed of joining the Harlem Globetrotters when he grew up. When Sinbad was in high school, he was a star on the school basketball team, played drums in a funk band, and wore his hair in a big red afro (red is Sinbad's natural hair color). Total strangers called him Red.

# Chapter 2
# Getting Laughs

Sinbad received a basketball scholarship to the University of Denver after he graduated from high school in 1974. "I had flaming red hair, and they called me 'Red Chamberlain.' I had 'Baby Wilt' [referring to the basketball legend Wilt Chamberlain] written on the side of my car. . . . I thought college ball was going to be the ticket," he says.

After he realized that he was never going to become a pro

**Sinbad graduated from high school in 1974.**

basketball player, he spent a few years in the U.S. Air Force. But he realized he wasn't cut out for the air force either, so after trying and losing several jobs—from doorman to waiter—Sinbad decided to try his hand at stand-up comedy. After all, his friends and family had always told him he was funny. In 1983, he launched what he calls his poverty tour, when he took his stand-up routine on the road. On this trip, he traveled by Greyhound bus to his destinations, working for meals and rooms along the way, often changing for his act in hotel restrooms.

Life on the road was hard. Once, before a gig in Dallas, he drove to the African-American radio station. He slept in his car all night, waiting for the station to open so that he could promote his comedy show that night. Sinbad says he wondered if he was going to make it. "I prayed, Please Lord, this is hard work, so if I'm not funny let me know right away."

After paying his dues on the road, he was chosen to appear on the mid-1980s television program *Star Search.* He ended up appearing on the show seven times and became a finalist, but he never won. He did win in a different way, though, because the comedian Redd Foxx, star of *Sanford and Son,* noticed him. Sinbad landed a role as Foxx's son on *The New Redd Foxx Show* in 1986. (He was also noticed by someone else: one of the people who voted on the show, David Salzman, brought in Sinbad to be host of the trendy talk show *Vibe* in 1997.)

In the mid-1980s, Sinbad appeared on the television show *Star Search.*

After *The New Redd Foxx Show,* Sinbad's next break came from famed comedian/actor Bill Cosby. Cosby loved Sinbad's hilarious, clean act. He asked him to appear on the TV show *A Different World,* a spinoff of the first *Cosby Show.* On this series, Sinbad played Walter, a basketball coach. Already Sinbad was starting to weave his real life into his acting and comedic life.

> **Sinbad never tells jokes. "I don't know any," he says.**

The man Oprah Winfrey calls "the funniest man on the planet" never tells jokes. "I don't know any," he says. Instead, Sinbad tromps around the stage, telling real stories that have happened to him and his family, adding a funny spin to everything. A large man (six feet five inches tall), his comedy is also large and physical. He moves around all the time. He dances, he gestures, he jumps—his big, dark eyes seem to pop out of his head. He acts out his characters in body language and mimics their voices. He pokes holes in everything normal people do—from running up credit cards to fighting with their wives to going to garage sales. He never writes down material, he just remembers it and relives it each time he performs.

*Below, Sinbad enjoys a peaceful moment.*

## Chapter 3
# Family Man

**Sinbad has two children who are a big part of his life.**

Married in the 1980s, Sinbad and his wife had two children: a daughter, Paige, born in 1984, and son, Royce, born in 1989. Sinbad and his wife divorced when the children were young.

"I expect a lot from you," Sinbad tells his kids. He takes them back to where he grew up, in Benton Harbor, Michigan, so that they can "see how life is." He tells them, "I jump on you harder than some of your friends because you have more."

As a divorced dad, Sinbad has joint custody of his children. They are a big part of his life, and fatherhood is very important to him. Since Sinbad seems to act like a big kid himself, he likes "just hanging" with his own children. He told *USA Weekend*, "We go to the library, to Chuck E Cheese's, to the movies. They go on the road with me. We play on computers. We watch videotapes. My kids are my partners. Also, I have rules [about my work]: No meetings in the morning because I take them to school, and after a certain time in the afternoon I won't take a meeting because I pick them up."

When it comes to child rearing, Sinbad believes that children need to be shown their limits. In his book, he says, "Parents now let their kids get away with too much.

**Every morning, Sinbad takes his children to school. Each afternoon, he picks them up.**

Kids today holler at their parents, go off on their parents, and their parents go, 'I don't know what to do.' You know what to do. You've just got to do it."

A big part of Sinbad's comic repertoire is about getting disciplined by his parents. "There were rules about whupping that every child knew. Number One: If you've got to get whupped, your father is the man. Mothers only whup you when they've lost their minds, and they don't stop until you're bleeding to death."

Even though he has some hilarious exaggerated bits about getting spanked, Sinbad the father avoids hitting his kids. "I try not to whup my kids," he writes. "I have come up with my own technique. I call it the *duct tape* way to peace and harmony with your child. If a kid

**"Mothers only whup you when they've lost their minds, and they don't stop until you're bleeding to death."**

acts up, duct tape them to the floor right where they are putting on a show," he jokes.

On a serious note, Sinbad is grateful for the guidance his parents gave him and tries to be the same kind of father to Paige and Royce. "My mother and father showed their love for me by showing me the boundaries, and I'm trying to do the same. That look my dad used to give me—I've developed that look," Sinbad told a writer for *USA Weekend*.

Keeping with the family spirit of things, he never curses in his performances. Sinbad says, "I want people to bring the whole family to my show." He emphasizes, "I work clean—no swearing, or sexy-clothes-wearing (because I can't fit into those tight pants)."

**"I want people to bring the whole family to my show. I work clean — no swearing, or sexy clothes-wearing."**

# Chapter 4
# Screen Star

In 1993, Sinbad was given his own variety comedy show, *The Sinbad Show*. Unfortunately, the show didn't last through one season. No matter: Sinbad was keeping busy enough with his live comedy performances and his budding movie career.

Sinbad's first bit part in a movie had been in *Club Med* in 1986, but his first meaty role was in the football comedy *Necessary Roughness* in 1991. Next were small parts in *Coneheads* (1993) and *Meteor*

**It was 1991 before Sinbad had a sub– stantial role in a movie.**

*Man* (1993), and a larger costarring role in *Houseguest* (1995), in which he played a clingy friend who wouldn't leave. His movie characters are usually genuine, friendly, yet goofy-acting guys. In *Jingle All the Way,* a 1996 Christmas movie that also starred Arnold Schwarzenegger, Sinbad played Myron Larabee, a crazed postman who is out to get the last Turbo Man toy on Christmas Eve before the distressed father Schwarzenegger.

But perhaps the best role Sinbad plays on film is himself, which he does masterfully in his taped comedy specials. One of the most successful of these, HBO's *Nothin' But the Funk,* aired in August 1997. These comedy videos capture his explosive energy and his manic and musical way of talking.

**The best role Sinbad plays on screen is himself.**

*Sinbad was at the Motown Cafe in Las Vegas, Friday, July 18, 1997, to kick off Sinbad's Soul Music Festival Tour. The tour featured some of the top musicians of the 1970s.*

To have more control over the products he makes, Sinbad formed his own production company, Afros and Bellbottoms Productions (named for his 1993 movie). It has produced two movies, including the HBO movie *The Cherokee Kid* and *First Kid*.

Besides appearing on the large and small screens, Sinbad still goes on the road with his stand-up act. Every year he lends his presence to Sinbad's Soul Music Festival in Aruba. This festival had its third anniversary in May 1998. It is an example of how much Sinbad loves everything about the '70s—the funk music, the huge Afros, platform shoes, and colorful clothes. He also went on a U.S. comedy tour with '70s group Earth, Wind & Fire in 1997. The popularity of *Sinbad's '70's Summer Jam*, a Memorial Day concert taped as an HBO special starting in 1995, testifies to the impact of the era's music.

**Sinbad loves everything about the '70s — the funk music, the huge Afros, platform shoes, and colorful clothes.**

## Chapter 5
# Reaching Out to Kids

**Sinbad helps kids in real life. He always finds time for volunteer service.**

In his more recent movie roles, Sinbad brings sense to the lives of children. He represents an adult who understands kids and who can give them real-world advice. In *First Kid* (1996), for example, he plays a Secret Service agent assigned to protect the 13-year-old son of the President of the United States. Critics said that Sinbad brought much-needed energy to the movie with his "goofy lug" act. In typical Sinbad fashion, the character doesn't act crude or use foul language. He's able to see through the boy's rebelliousness and realize he is lonely and needs lessons on how to be "cool." Disguised as a cup of Coke and falling into birthday cakes, he becomes a hero to the boy, wising him up to how to handle bullies and let people know his feelings.

*Sinbad helped out at the Kids Race Against Drugs in April 1998.*

But besides helping kids in the movies, Sinbad also helps kids in real life. He finds time for volunteer work, especially with community services that affect children. Working with the Children's Defense Fund (an advocacy group for poor, minority, and disabled children in the United States) and the Omega Boys Club has kept him aware of children's

*Sinbad appeared on the 1997 Nickelodean Kid's Choice Awards.*

needs. For the Children's Defense Fund, he cohosted the *National House Party* in 1995 with actor Danny Glover. This program was a national telecast on behalf of the Black Community Crusade for Children (BCCC), broadcast on Black Entertainment Television (BET).

Sinbad accompanied First Lady Hillary Rodham Clinton on a 1996 trip to war-torn Bosnia, where he provided comic relief to U.S. peacekeeping forces. He also performed a concert at Morehouse College, the proceeds of which benefited the Endowed Scholarship Fund in the names of his parents, the Reverend Donald and Louise Adkins. His commitment to AIDS awareness inspired his participation in the *Time Out* video benefiting the Magic Johnson Foundation.

Once, Sinbad was touring the Virgin Islands in the Caribbean when Hurricane Hugo hit the island of St. John. Sinbad volunteered to help clean up in the storm's aftermath. Spending time there, helping out, caused him to adopt the island of St. John. "I fell in love with St. John because I

**In 1996, Sinbad traveled to war-torn Bosnia where he provided comic relief to U.S. peace–keeping forces.**

thought it was like the Old West with its barn raisings. I thought it was charming," he told a St. John journalist, describing the community spirit of rebuilding after the hurricane.

Sinbad loves computers. He's a fan of the Apple Macintosh and has owned a Mac in one form or another since 1986. Extremely computer literate, he'd like to set up after-school computer learning centers across the country. He believes that equipping kids with information and computer skills prepares them for life. Two of his favorite Web sites are "Everything Black" and "Black Geeks Online."

**Sinbad loves computers. He is an avid Apple Mac fan.**

## Chapter 6
# The Show Must Go On

In 1997, Sinbad published his book, which is a combination of his autobiography and stand-up routines, called *Sinbad's Guide to Life: Because I Know Everything.* As to why he wrote the book, he believes he is a big know-it-all, and as he told a writer for *USA Weekend,* "Give me a subject and I'll give you an answer."

He dedicated his book "To every goofy, uncool kid out there somewhere in the world.

**Sinbad likes to joke that he is a big know-it-all.**

Remember, hang in there. It's going to be all right." Sinbad still identifies with the "goofy, uncool" kid he once was and has sympathy for what kids go through while they're growing up.

From October 1997 until mid-1998, Sinbad served as host of the late-night talk show *Vibe* on the WB Network. He was the second host of the one-hour show. He was larger, louder, and more famous than his predecessor, Chris Spencer.

When E! Online asked him why he thought he was selected to replace Spencer on *Vibe*, Sinbad guessed it was because he appeals to young and old viewers alike. "You don't have to be young to catch a young audience. I saw Red Skelton; I see Chris Rock. I'm old and young. I'm like Dick Clark."

**Sinbad still identifies with the "goofy, uncool kid" he says he once was.**

As always, his style as talk-show host was characteristically warmhearted. He had fun poking fun—at himself and at others. Sporting a huge smile with what looks like 400 teeth, he was a hip, hyper, and caring host. He liked to get guests on his show who were "trying to make a difference."

Throughout his life, Sinbad has made a difference. Both his comic appearances and volunteer work have affected young and old alike.

**Sinbad appeals to young and old audiences alike. His routines are timeless.**

## Sinbad's Works

**Television appearances:**
*Star Search* (mid-1980s)
*The New Redd Foxx Show* (1986)
*Keep on Cruisin'* (1987)
*A Different World* (1987)
*The Sinbad Show* (1993)
Hosted the 1996 *Essence* Awards
*Nothin' But the Funk* (1997)
*Sinbad's '70's Summer Jam* (late 1990s)
Host of *Vibe* (October 1997–1998)

**Movies and TV Movies:**
*Club Med* (1986)
*That's Adequate* (1989)
*Hot Shots!* (1991)
*Necessary Roughness* (1991)

*Movies (Cont'd)*
*The Meteor Man* (1993)
*Sinbad: Afros and Bellbottoms* (1993)
*Happily Ever After: Fairy Tales for Every Child* (1995)
*Houseguest* (1995)
*The Cherokee Kid* (HBO; 1996)
*Jingle All the Way* (1996)
*First Kid* (1996)
*Good Burger* (1997)

**Comedy CDs:**
*Brain Damaged* (1990)
*Sinbad's Guide to Life* (1997)

# Chronology

- Born David Adkins on November 10, 1956, in Benton Harbor, Michigan, to the Reverend Donald Adkins and Louise Adkins
- 1974, received a basketball scholarship to the University of Denver
- In 1983, after a stint in the air force, became a stand-up comedian and worked for years on the road until he was discovered on television show *Star Search*
- Married and had two children: daughter, Paige, born in 1985 and son, Royce, born in 1989
- 1986, started his TV career as a regular on the Bill Cosby–produced *A Different World*
- 1991, movie role in *Necessary Roughness*
- 1996, won the Blockbuster Entertainment Award for favorite supporting actor for *Jingle All the Way*
- 1997, went on a U.S. comedy tour with '70s artists, including the band Earth, Wind & Fire
- 1997-1998, host for late-night talk show on the WB Network called *Vibe*

# Index